Copyright © 2023

Don't forget to leave us **Your Feedback!**

This Book Belongs To:

_____

_____

I Spy with my little eye
Something beginning with ...

Apple

I Spy with my little eye
Something beginning with ...

Boots

I Spy with my little eye
Something beginning with ...

C

Carols

I Spy with my little eye
Something beginning with ...

Deer

I Spy with my little eye
Something beginning with ...

Earmuff

I Spy with my little eye
Something beginning with ...

F

Firewood

I Spy with my little eye
Something beginning with ...

Gloves

I Spy with my little eye
Something beginning with ...

Hockey

I Spy with my little eye
Something beginning with ...

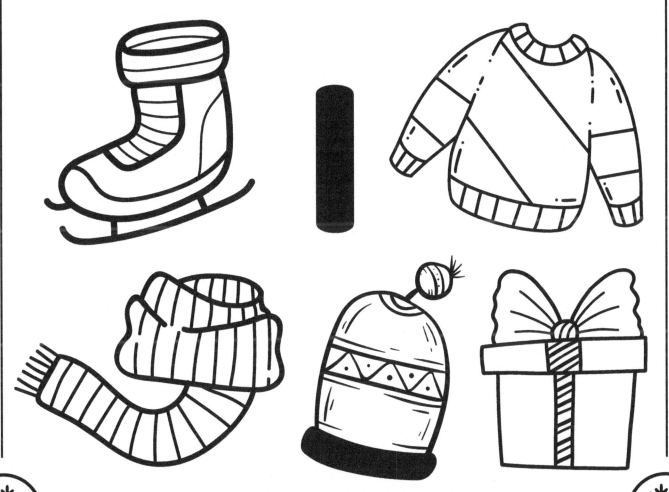

Ice skate

I Spy with my little eye
Something beginning with ...

Jacket

Jacket

I Spy with my little eye
Something beginning with ...

K

Kite

I Spy with my little eye
Something beginning with ...

L

Luge

I Spy with my little eye
Something beginning with ...

Mittens

I Spy with my little eye Something beginning with ...

Nest

I Spy with my little eye
Something beginning with ...

O

Owl

I Spy with my little eye
Something beginning with ...

Pinecone

I Spy with my little eye
Something beginning with ...

Queen

I Spy with my little eye
Something beginning with ...

Reindeer

I Spy with my little eye
Something beginning with ...

Scarf

I Spy with my little eye
Something beginning with ...

Teddy bear

I Spy with my little eye Something beginning with ...

Umbrella

I Spy with my little eye
Something beginning with ...

Vestments

I Spy with my little eye
Something beginning with ...

Wood stove

I Spy with my little eye
Something beginning with ...

Xylophone

I Spy with my little eye
Something beginning with ...

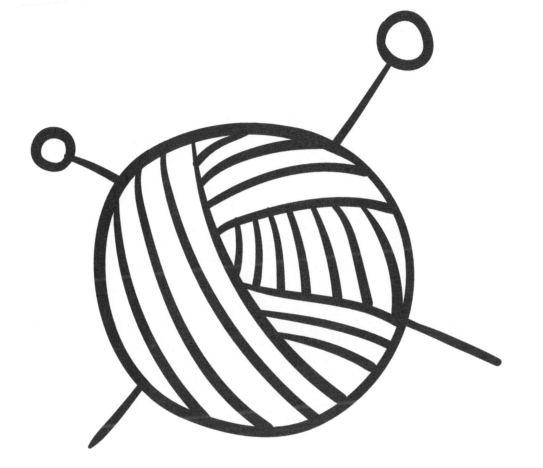

Yarn

I Spy with my little eye
Something beginning with ...

Zebra

WINTER
Time

I hope you enjoyed ♡
Support our work by leaving us
Good Feedback!
Discover more fun books in
Our store "Flora Wenna"

Made in United States
Orlando, FL
21 October 2024